An environmentally friendly book printed and bound in England by
www.printondemand-worldwide.com

This book is made entirely of chain-of-custody materials

ii

ISBN 978-178035-675-4

First published 2013 by
FASTPRINT PUBLISHING
Peterborough, England.

reader in an accessible manner. This ability is not universally found, and even those who claim to be poets are unable to make their true feelings clear to a lay reader. This is one of the reasons why many school children find it difficult to empathise with poems that are either abstruse or jargon-laden. There are, however, exceptions; sometimes, good poetry comes from the pen of those who have no pretensions to the skills of poetic writing. One such person is Mahesh Godbole of Rochdale, a retired eye specialist who, for thirty years, promoted in the north west of England the best of Indian music under the aegis of the Indian Classical Music Society that he founded in 1976.

In this fifth series of his poetic works Godbole presents poems that combine passion and intimacy. Not a

A one bull open cart
Sturdy and smart
Pulled along the street

A man got down. Raced up the steps
My father to meet
Produced he a chit
From a white Sahib
A Sahib of no rank, I have to be frank.
'A superb show'. It read
With a scribbly sign.
A price was decided.
He waved, the rest descended
They unloaded their things to no end
Long poles to small gadgets.

All said, what followed, didn't testify his claim. Sat amidst
the listeners.
Was a Sanskrit scholar. To point at him a finger of blame.
Some names of Gods. Were attributes of other Lords!
The Sanskrit pronunciation. Unworthy of appreciation.

To fool all he thought, he had a good stock
Yet he himself made up for a laughing stock.

In the poem *Give Them their Due* Godbole, a staunch Marathi nationalist and patriot, recounts some of the virtues and benefits the British brought to India; and, in a swipe at the existing haphazard system of government, reminds us that the British

If that be life. A thing that moves.

A curfew in peace!

An old lady not seen. For a week.

In a similar vein, the poem *Where else?* talks of the land of haves and have nots in which beggars and homeless people flourish. One of them calls himself a lonely loony. On the other hand, in the poem *Salutation*, Godbole touches upon the most intractable social problem confronting Britons: alcohol and drug-induced violence of the youth. His respect for the British police is palpable:

Hats off to the British Constabulary.

Will gain oral wealth
Add many a word by stealth
Not unlike the Raj
It will grow and grow.

The third group of poems brings out Godbole's observations on aspects of human nature, particularly human frailties. In the poem *Money Matters* the hesitant would-be philanthropist promises to change the world once he has the money, but on securing some money postpones his promise until he gets more, and so on. In the end, all he is interested is in getting better returns on his bets. The poem *Friends* talks of how we fail to retain the friends we start off with when we are young:

She feeds me, cleans me
and dresses me too.
I never need to woo.

In the poem *Lines on Rudyard* Godbole ruminates on the rise and fall of literary reputations, as in the case of Rudyard Kipling, who wrote much and yet, on return to England, was not heeded much as a poet:

Leaned your balance on weight
Not on value.
A common trap for common writers.

Another reflective poem is *The Chessboard*. Here, the character and desires of individuals are observed in what

Loyalty?

The last category of Godbole's poems contains those that are intensely personal, and tinged with sorrow. Deep-seated depression and suicide are the dominant themes of two poems. In *Survival of the Wicked* Godbole laments the loss of a dear family friend, Nigel, who took his own life. The poignant first verse echoes his sadness:

Tell me Nigel, what lay behind that three storey laughter
The one we were ever after
And the joy it brought
How didn't it forever last?

But ... I am a trained dissector
Of things post-humus.

Don’t turn in the grave
The poems are dark as the cave
Wherein they lie.400 of 600.

No wonder ,on return to England
They didn’t heed you much, as ,a poet.

Leaned your balance on weight
Not on value.
A common trap for common writers.

Lived you to a mature age. You didn’t grow up
Else lapsed into boyhood with tarralums and

No human soul.
Cats roam round
A postman on his round
A stray car hisses around
If that be life .A thing that moves.

Oh boy.
The back gates shake hands in a storm
To cause a flutter .
The single contact, if it matters, with thy neighbour.

Lights lit in the houses.
Within. Business as usual.

A curfew in peace!

Now at eighty as a Hindu conformist
I return to Him.

To ask Him humbly

Is thy other name not Wishful Thinking

deprivation are parts
Of the same entity. Humanity. Atop the second storey.To it the
Instance relates in this story.

The Head Master shaves for the coming day,in the fading light.
His two daughters are back home, after a game of table tennis
I, their cousin was sat on a chair.

Fast on their heels enters a lad of twenty. Plainly attired.A cotton bag
Hangs down his shoulder. My uncle casts a glance of hope.
Yet another private tuition!

The girls recognise him .
A street actor .

'Well done.
Truly professional '
I exclaim.

Yet many waited to creep. And to gossip kept they
Their attentive ears. Have you heard the one about
The Scotsman? etc.

They came to blows. As bottles and glasses flowed.
As a dispute over drugs arose.Police arrived. As the culprits
Fled off the road. In fear and fury. Soon two Bobbies
Overpowered the gang of three. It was no fun .To do it
Without a gun. Chained they the three with hands at the back.
In the van packed them on the track.

Hats off to the British Constabulary.
Trained and alert. To nip trouble in the bud. To avert

Of the many, Havan nearer to heaven is a dear one.

In this day and age It's time to turn our back to Him. Despite
I was asked to attend a Havan. Lit was the fire to quench the
Ire of Gods all. Made to measure the needs of believers all.

The fire was lit. The smoke our breaths bit. Few windows opened.
The cold wind swept in. The young Guru got up as on the screen.
Announced his credential. Much as a comic commercial.

The Guru's expertise spread with age and pedantry.

A cherubian face of devotion and calm.

On the nine leaves of beetle nuts, rested nine
Beetle nuts-icon of Gods. Time to time the host
Put a pound .As the priest wetted with a salt-spoon
Of water and uttered Namaha Swaha.

Then appealed he to all assembled, to make a contribution
“It was all in the holy script.” Tell me another, thought I.
Courtesy held me from causing a rift. I for one a total atheist
Simply bowed and left.

Fact travels faster than gossip

But now a new breed is born
To take up those pages.

Please. .....Read on.

Long past my hearing

With passing years
Two rice noodles
Peep out of my ears.
To overhear.
Eavesdrop.

On the daughter- in- law
Who is plotting
Behind closed doors.

The bidding didn't end soon.
Light gave way to light.
A freshening breeze bucked up a kite
Not to its full height

A one bull open cart
Sturdy and smart
Pulled along the street

A man got down. Raced up the steps
My father to meet
Produced he a chit
From a white Sahib
A Sahib of no rank. I have to be frank.
'A superb show' .It read
With a scribbly sign.

All a child's play for them.
For us hey for hey. A treat on treat yet a
Backward leap, to dangle from the rope
Was a remarkable feat. four adults stretched out
A white, pressed sheet, just in case.

Back to earth, the kids displayed varied acrobats
You could miss if your lids dropped.

Countless turns in turns on a single hand
Worth an applause on a band
Within a twinkle of an eye
The sizable girl got in and out of a narrow
Iron ring. Then a Naag peeped out of a box
Swayed it with the tune of a flute. As children we
Were amused and mute. Ignorant all, that

It began with a bang
And ended in a clang
Of steel chains. Round
Their wrists.

Now I have some to spare
I Say I SHALL if I have more.

Try I the Lotto.
To raise my motto.

Should fortune smile
I shall say .wait a while

And ask
Where do I get the best returns?

I don't ask for many.
For me. A lonely loony.

Can't cope with corruption
It now leaves no option
In this land of haves and have nots.

Welcome.Visitor,
Can you spare me a penny?

My better half, helps the dead half.
She feeds me ,cleans me
and dresses me too.
I never need to woo.

Turns me for bedsore
Cry I no more.
Oft to temper
I give vent to
Who else can I turn to? save the dark death?

Never ever. No fag.
No drink.Yet wait I
To be pushed over
The edge for ever.

I thank fate. To leave my brain
A timely mate.

Shows off his
'creation'
times untold.

A pupil at school
shines with merit
Broadcasts he all
To his credit.

An officer is
Raised to a
Higher rank
Tells he all
Proud and frank.

Age ripens

The range of his pace
The leap of his faculty
To face in face
Of difficulty.

Is he a pawn
Not to look back
But to look fore
More and more.

Or the long range
Camel is he? kicked
To run over the vast
Land.

A knight to jump

A trusted
Loyalty?

You sink
Or sustain

The flood
Of people
from beyond

ENGLISH

Not unlike the Thames
English will never dry
Will never overflow
But gently gain
Rivulets.

As the colonel in Sudan!

Time will tell.

Along a long fury road.
My mind slumped into melancholy
My foot fell into a depression.
Roped it in many more,
Economic, volcanic, Tsunamic
And worse mental.

To mark the bottom line
BIPOLAR.
When logic departs and madness sets in
The two poles not far apart

Down in the dumps
Up in the clouds

Parents terrorised by either

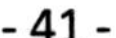

Honoured they you

Not with cash but kind
Cutlery , cards and
Many many things
Came your way

Many , many things
Came your way
From the bird sanctuary.

Like a kite , float I gaily
With all my might,
Height on height .

Until cruel fate
Snips my life line
The umbilical chord .

Up above, the cloudy
Water bag, bursts.
A storm blows.

And I land to find
A burial ground .
Yes. A burial ground
And I hear, a death knell sound!

Who was the silent dreamer?
Who else but Tendulkar?

Players and viewers alike
Knew it was coming to fruition
From 99th they gave him
And him alone, a standing ovation

His 100th century was worth a watch
Gritty pursuit in each stroke of the match.
He went in with a loaded gun
Fired well past the target runs on run
The envious said “The opponent was a small fry”
Said I, “Just as England was for Ireland.”

Critics quoted it aloud.
To a reminder they bowed
Against Sachin's 200, NOT OUT.

They went their ways
A few fell by byways
Some chose to disown ,others too famed to be known
The rest for reasons unknown.

A few chose to live alone
Some tend to bemoan

A few I could'nt cope
For burdens of my own.

Now if you ask
I am left, with 2 steadfast,

Stand they in the shadow

Or a primi- para her baby.

Your window on the world, the door too
Crystal clear he leaves
To pry on the neighbour's
Goings on. For him to look
In , save a few corners
To escape his eagle eye.

Are we tidy or shabby
Dirty or clean? Clothes
Scattered? curtains dusted
Bed made. Is it by a maid?
House clinically clean
Ornaments or lights,
Tests he our taste

How did'nt it forever last?

What mortgage, what loans ,or unceasing enmity?
What likes and dislikes or absurd
Reality not new to mankind?

A mere game of poker you largely won
Left him with a mounting grudge?
Played he his game,
Your name to smudge.
Poured he a generous
Peg on peg!

On the way home, to your surprise
The Police your arrival hailed
The breath test you failed.

Yet a Hindu at heart
With faith in afterlife.

Tell me Nigel, what lay behind the cheery laughter
The one we were ever after.
And the joy it brought
How did'nt it for ever last?

The dream off
His eyes with
Velvety soft Layered clouds.

Praised too have they the sinking sun, sapped of
Might. Ending a day of
It's flight ,over
The mighty globe.

Yet few have turned
Their eye to meet
The midday fiery
Glow that burns
The ire and ego
Of White batsmen.

ND - #0271 - 080726 - C0 - 197/132/5 - PB - 9781780356754 - Gloss Lamination